Adult Coloring Book

Butterflies #2

ISBN-13: 978-1532743344

ISBN-10: 1532743343

All enquiries, contact

Hobby Habitat Coloring

contact@hobbyhabitat.com

Get a FREE Coloring Book

Coloring book fan?

Get a free coloring book from the website bellow:

www.hobbyhabitat.com/freecoloringbook

Hello and thank you for buying and coloring our latest adult coloring book!

This is our second butterflies book; we just can't get enough of these lovely creatures so we have included 50 high definition butterfly images for you to color.

As before we have included a range of designs, from easier ones up to what you could call "expert level" designs, so no matter if you are a novice or experienced colorist you will find design suitable for your need.

We hope that you will enjoy coloring these wonderful stress relieving patterns as much as we enjoyed putting them together for you.

Once again thank you for buying our book, and enjoy coloring with Hobby Habitat's adult coloring books.

Thank you!

Hobby Habitat Coloring Books

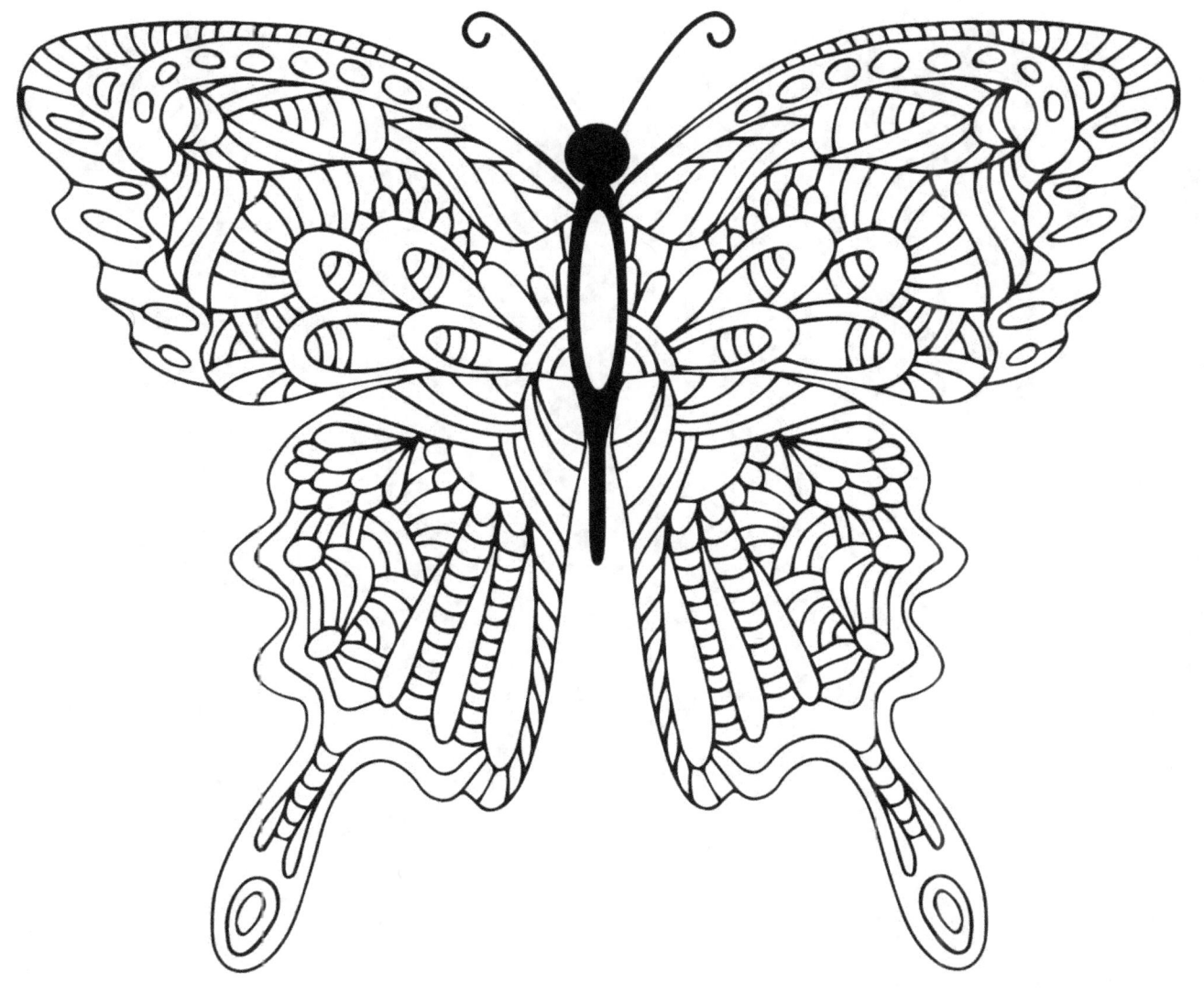

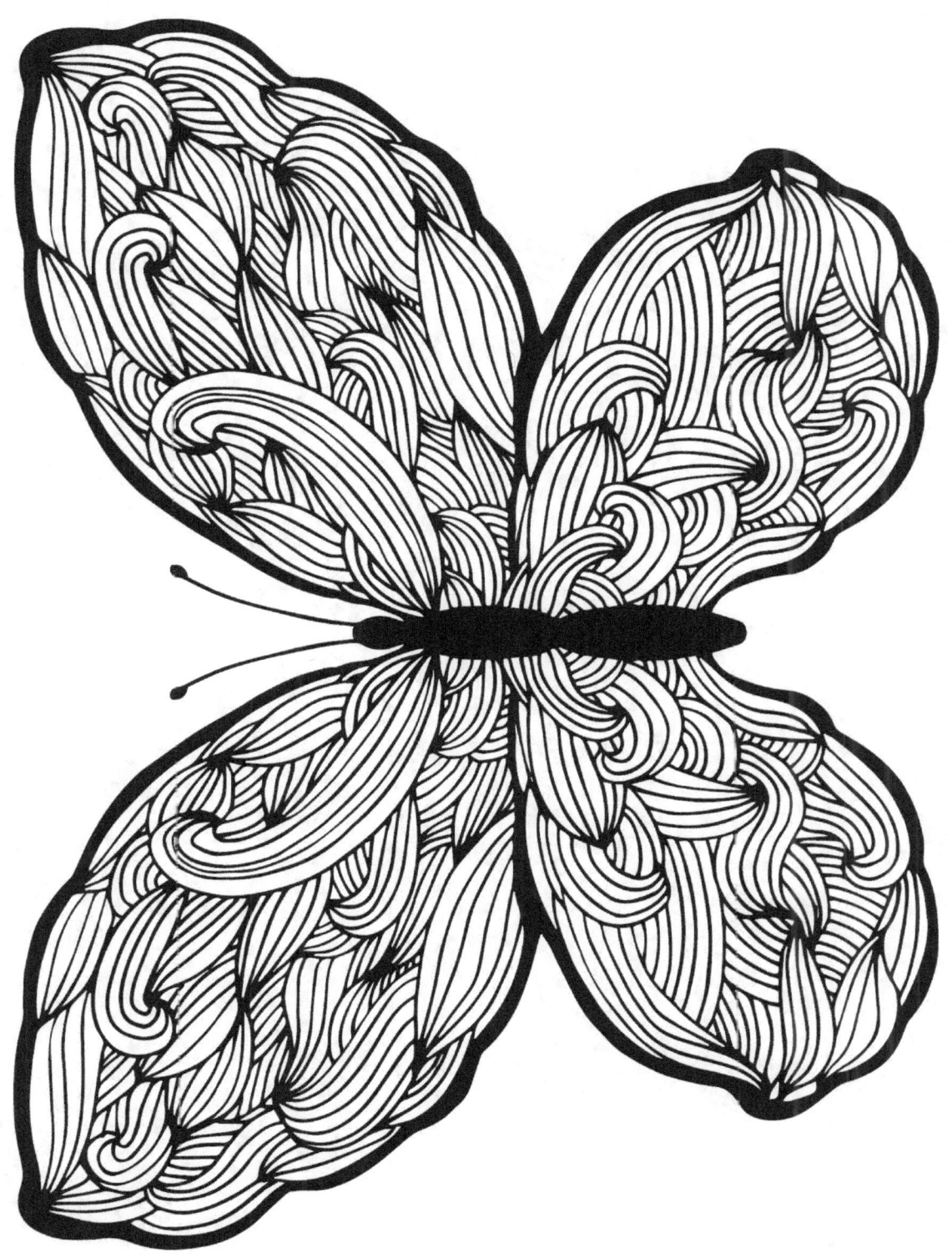

More books from Hobby Habitat

You can find our entire Coloring Books collection on Amazon, just type in

"Hobby Habitat Coloring Books"

in the search box…or *search* for the books bellow by ISBN number!

ISBN: 1522839542   ISBN: 1523607149

ISBN: 1523617411

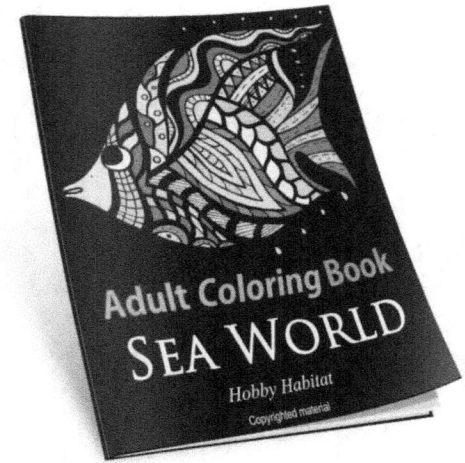

ISBN: 1523608544

ISBN: 1519755589

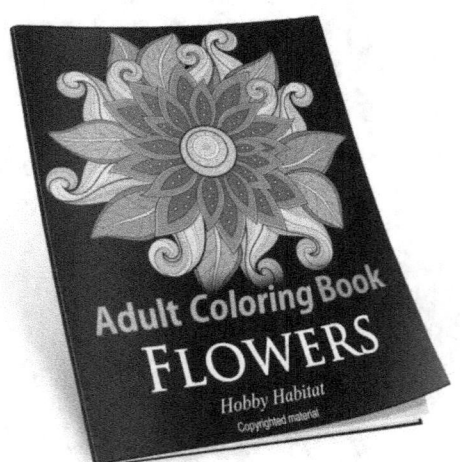

ISBN: 1523898917

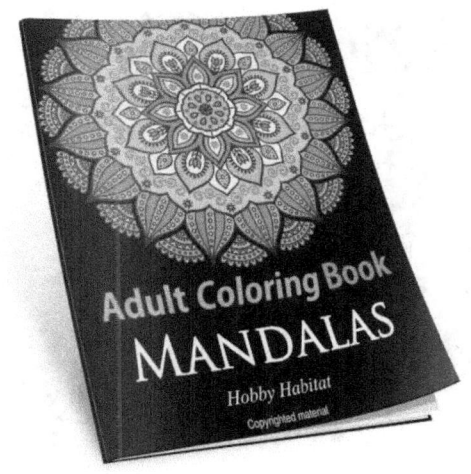

ISBN: 152389900X

ISBN: 1530035554

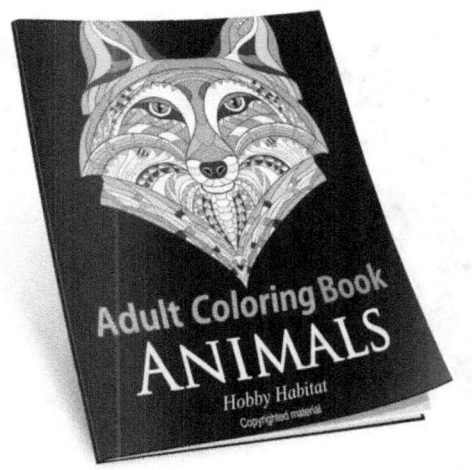

ISBN: 1530035473

ISBN: 1530660955

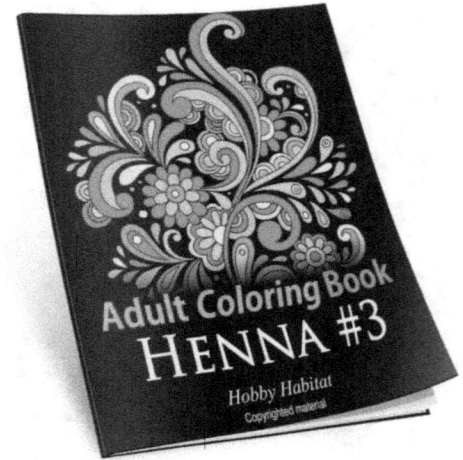

ISBN: 1532707762

ISBN: 1532708459

ISBN: 1532725485

From the Author

Thank you for buying and coloring our book, we sincerely hope you have enjoyed it!

Can we ask for a small favor? A lot of work goes in to preparing and publishing our books and honest reviews really do help us, especially when it comes to understanding what we should improve in our books.

If you have a minute, we would really appreciate if you could go to the book store where you have purchased this book and leave a short review…we do actually read our reviews!

Thank you!

Remember also to grab your FREE bonus book at:

www.hobbyhabitat.com/freecoloringbook

www.ingramcontent.com/pod-product-compliance
Lightning Source LLC
Chambersburg PA
CBHW081553280526
45788CB00011B/3463